101 Poems
and Philosophies for
Geezers and Geezerettes

101 Poems and Philosophies for Geezers and Geezerettes

Mary Elizabeth Burgess

authorHOUSE®

AuthorHouse™ LLC
1663 Liberty Drive
Bloomington, IN 47403
www.authorhouse.com
Phone: 1-800-839-8640

Cover credit: "Balloons" by Marie Wenner

Published by AuthorHouse   12/17/2013

ISBN: 978-1-4918-4161-7 (sc)
ISBN: 978-1-4918-4163-1 (hc)
ISBN: 978-1-4918-4162-4 (e)

Library of Congress Control Number: 2013922431

Contents

Prescription

"To ponder what life means
Precipitates sickness," the doctor said.
"Not to," the patient replied,
"Means you're nearly dead.
"It's not the asking makes one ill,
But expecting answers will.

"If they come, they are the gifts
Of birds whose songs the gray dawn lifts."
                    Pub. in *George Street Carnival,* 1972, and *Gifts*, 1986

Inventions for Oldsters

This is true (at least the first part).
Airbags for walkers so you can play
Michelin Man and Pillsbury Doughboy
when you trip or bump needlessly.

Hearing aids that glow in the dark in case
you have to answer a two a.m. call.

Rusty joints for hips, knees, shoulders
for built-in malpractice cases.

The baby boomers are making mints off us.
But they need to invent:
sweetly-scented Beano,
nose—and ear-hair clippers with platinum handles, and
multi-colored Depends for multi-colored ingestions.

A Husband's Lament

The cause of E. D. is grandchildren.

Those wees, the threes, rouse you to wee,
and who can get it on or off when there's three
in your bed. They age, as do you, but by then they'll
want to know what grown-ups do behind closed doors.

Parents can close doors, but not grandparents.
Oh, no, they'd rather be dead than lock out
a dearly beloved grandchild.

In inverse proportion your passion has gone out of fashion
as theirs is coming into.
It's been so long since you made love
you've forgotten how to.
Your face'd be red if you even tried to cuddle in bed.

What's a guy for?
By now you've forgotten. But hey, there's help—ta-da!

Viagra to the rescue!
If it's good enough for Dole, it's good enough for you.

So get up! Get going! Say, "Get into bed, pardner—
you're burning daylight."
Just pop that pill with a swill of red wine,
get the blood pumpin', you'll be sumpin',
by the time it's 'leven—quick now—
before the little one's seven.

There'll come a time when the tide will turn:
the little ones will become bigger ones,
and they'll have their own little ones—oh, sure,
they will make love, till *their* little ones
sleep between *them*.

Meantime, buy Viagra, go to Niagara, pop it nightly
before your wife turns unsightly.

Pray.

Advice from the Alzheimer's Association

Get plenty of mental stimulation: read, do puzzles,
learn a new language or hobby, go to the theater,
listen to CD's, travel.

Exercise: dance, walk or jog, walk (in water or in land)
or swim (in water), practice low-impact calisthenics,

Enjoy a healthy diet: fresh fruits and green, leafy vegetables
(but you don't have to become a vegan),
legumes—peas, beans, nuts, seeds, fish, low-fats,
ice cream with real fat only twice a week.

Share, enjoy, create, be kind, be curious, love
and be passionate about something.

When They Do the Autopsy

They'll think he rode horses from the spurs on his vertebrae,
lived in Battle Creek, Michigan, for the snap-crackle-pops in his
neck, produced bad records for Sony
from the condition of his discs, and went fishing every day
from the rods in his back.

An autopsy can tell a lot, especially on the guy who really
knew how to live, even when he's got saddle-sores,
ulcers, hernias, and flounders almost every day.

A Podiatrist

's job is hard.
It's hard to cut nails that are not soft,
dig ingrowns from toes that are not hard,
rub callouses the right way.

So treat him softly: he's worth every *scen*t.

Blueberries Are Good For the Brain

Brains contain millions, billions, infinite
(because they're infinitesimal) numbers of neurons,
those message containers, carriers, de-coders, connecting
with dendrites and axons at either end, not really connecting
because the synapses—gaps, nothing—are a marvel,
allowing plasticity, continuous re-mapping
of the brain and its memories,
and actual generation of new neurons.
Think of it!
Grey matter, a blob of image from Image
breathing life into the universe.

History Lessons

The radio brings tears with news in '56 of the Salk vaccine—
no polio for my little boy!
and again, in '62 tears of joy with John Glenn's space flight.

With t.v. in '69 at night all four of us open our eyes
and hardly talk of the marvelous walk Armstrong makes
on the moon.

In no time soon our two will be in television and medicine—
as camera man and 'lectrician!

The Economy

We are worried.

Margie, my friend's sister,
is afraid she'll lose her house,
though it's almost paid for.

So I sent her Keith's "rules of the road"
for such perilous times: —diversify, diversify, diversify,
his battle cry for investing at any time—
when markets are volatile, buy precious metals,
gold and silver, platinum and uranium
acceptable as well

—know what's in your mutual funds—
don't buy "junk bonds"

—in retirement, balance evenly
between stocks and bonds (with gold on the side),
the percentage depends on who's president
and what your nerves can stand

—don't listen to the news every day, and especially
don't follow your investments every day
(unless you're sure they're leading you down
a primrose Wall Street)

—pray a lot.

Finally, Margie, if you lose your house,
you can live with me, and if I lose mine,
I'll live with you. We bi-polars have to stick together.

Things to Do Before I Die

—Ride in a convertible with the top down*
(have already ridden on a motorcycle twice
and liked the wind in my hair, the freedom)

—Walk in the rain without an umbrella,
my face turned to the heavens*
—Dig in the dirt again and plant something*
—Swim with no clothes on—no-no!—
I don't need to do that again!
—Cook a full-course meal for twelve once more
—Be in the movies (I was on t.v.
three times and a Blog once)

—Rob a bank—*not*

—Peel onions without crying

—Stand on my head again (I tried this recently,
but I couldn't get my backside up)

—Tumble in the circus, and walk the high wire

—Go to a Bruce Springsteen concert

—Own and drive a pink Cadillac convertible,
although an Atomic Blue Civic sedan works just as well

> And *after* I die,
> the possibilities,
> the freedom,
> the possibilities are endless . . .

*Did these at 76

Age-Old Bonds

No sense "This hurts me more than it hurts you."
I felt the sting of wood and didn't want to sit just yet.

Now I tie restraints binding flesh to wood.
You sit yet yet yet, no sense.
This hurt stings me-not-you.

Catacombs

Cavernous doors swing open at a touch,
indifferent outdoor air is sucked up
by medicine-urine-carnation smells.
Foam-padded plush carpeting traps
the light, hurried step which moves
through Empire-furnitured lounges—
a few vital heads nod greeting—
down the long hallway chandeliered like some
grand merciful terminal
wide enough for spoked chariots
going nowhere with their twisted bodies whose gravity
strains against restraining bands, past these wall slots
filled with skeletons on lively jacquard slabs.
Cadaverous faces, flesh worn thin from bones within,
and staring unseeing eyes in hollow spaces haunt.

Some distant spectral moan like Cybil lures
me to my weekly ritual,
to my warm corpse, remembrance of a suckled past,
whose ghostly smile and disembodied words,
stabbed with memory's shards—
before the grave sleep comes—
taunt.

Pub.in *Gifts*. 1986

Good Heavens!

I forgot to put my earrings on and Emeraude
to remember her by,
she who instructed me never to wear red shoes or panties—
"trashy," you know.

Today I'm wearing both in memory:
I saw her buy red shoes once—
it made her more and more alive.

Gardening

At six I grew daffodils and tulips and sweet peas
—so hard to grow and train to climb those strings,
but so sweet, and sweet mother knew I'd love them.

We had two Victory Gardens, one in our small backyard
and one a few blocks away behind the school
when I was nine to thirteen, growing tomatoes and peas,
green and yellow beans (when the rabbits didn't nibble)
and weeds (the critters never minded them).

When I married, I grew tomatoes—always tomatoes, Big Boys
because they're early—and petunias, geraniums, bulbs
of every type, rhododendron and azaleas
(with husband's help), mint, parsley, chives, basil,
wild garlic and wild onion.

Tiger lilies, daylilies needing dead-heading,
And Madonna lilies (the bulbs from Mother)
abounded at one time.
Roses—that's another story (Momma always grew
such gorgeous ones in spite of aphids, mildew,
and hurricanes). The roses went, of their own accord.

With children, came sunflowers.
"They feed the birds this winter, honeyboy, and sure,
you can help plant the seeds."
My, how they grew, and grew, and g-r-e-w!
Honey was amazed, even more so when the cardinals,
blue jays, and robins came to the feast.

Later at another house came the trumpet vine,
blaring its orange way up my chimney,
yews, junipers, pyracantha—till we got tired of the thorns,
eunomous (firebush) and spirea (bridal veil).
Yarrow and Queen Anne's lace (this from the roadside)
to be dried and hung on the December tree.

Other roadside yields: stalks in the fall
to dry for winter's glory.
Surprise! they yielded insects—
flying insects emerging unbidden.

African violets were Mother's specialty.
She divided them, started "babies,"
gave them light on the chipped,
yellowed kitchen windowsills facing north.
How many times did she give me babies, too,
saying, just not too much light or too much water.
Nevertheless my babies died, one by one,
though I tried to follow her prescription.
Now at seventy-five, there's magenta clematis
climbing my lamppost in late May, early June,
(the talk of the neighborhood!)
and houseplants—yes, honey, there's plenty of *them*.
They don't require kneeling in the dirt, weeding, seeding,
watering only once a week and not much light—
philodendron, pothos, peace lily.
Ivy's good in and out (use nicotine liquid or coffee to control
aphids; you know you have them when white dust
shows on the dark endtable).
Corn and rubber plants. Shefflera requires much light
so it does well under skylights or in sunrooms.
I know it's a jungle, honeyboy, but I don't expect
to ever get to Africa, so why can't I have my own?

Oh—and I have an African violet now. Doing nicely,
thank you, because, from honeygirl, my daughter-in-law,
it's artificial!

Scents and the Advertising Industry

Peach in hand cream, roses I splash on my arms,
citrus in shampoo, coconut in conditioner.

Those guys in advertising would have us believe
all's right with the world if we just use the right scent.
Clever names, too: Degree, Arrid, Ban.

Mr. Jergens gave me my best Scent Memory:
rosewood and almond rubbed into my consciousness
as she rubbed it into her hands, smooth and creamy,
a gift that's lasted for my seventy-seven years.

I find it on the supermarket shelf,
but it's never advertised anymore.
There's no need when the logo and product
are permanently embedded:
rosewood and almond,
rosewood and almond.

Sundae Forgiveness

"Turn the heat up. Button your sweaters tight."
It's Sunday: must be ice cream night!
For creamy cold vanilla, Brother goes to the store
while I help Mother
stir dusty cocoa into yellow melted butter.
She pours crystal-white sugar, slowly adds water.
Bubbles form and break, chased by heat
in this syrupy, cold winter night's treat.

Brother bursts the door. "Time to eat!"
He sets out plates, begins to dip.
But the hot pan slips my grip, then flips.
Dark brown silk runs down the wall.
Though now the ice cream won't wear chocolate,
Mother serves the smoothest, sweetest words of all:
"Don't cry. You didn't mean to do it."

Twenty-Fifth Anniversary

Once our love was shiny and bright like silver.
We thought it pure, hard, durable,
and put it too many times in closets,
bringing it out occasionally to remove surface tarnish
so it could reflect what we thought
love should be.

No strange alchemy here, but now,
from our separate crucibles come elements—
baser than shiny silver dreams,
yet precious nevertheless—
creating the malleable softness of fine pewter.
Uncloseted it can wear the dents and scratches
of the years gracefully, its inner strength
coming from what love is.

Battle of the Sexes

Ladies, Wives, Mothers vs. Gentlemen, Husbands, Fathers

"To a lovely lady" he wrote on the flyleaf
of the book of poems he gave to her.
"To my wonderful wife for buttons sewed
favors bestowed and a clean abode"
said last year's anniversary card.

"Thank you for being the mother
of my children" were his parting words.
Some words of hurt hurt
less than some words of appreciation.
"Well done thou good and faithful servant."

    Ladies and Gentlemen
    Wives and Husbands
    Mothers and Fathers
    let your selves be persons
    man and woman

Monday

On Monday the refrigerator hissed its good-bye.
On Monday the Chevvie died: I was late to work.
On Monday the mechanic said $97 for a fuel pump,
$43 for a cable, $285 for new brake lining.
Plus labor.

On Monday the doorknob came off in my hand.
On Monday the courthouse sent the final papers.
On Monday evening a pretzel broke my front tooth.
One more surprise, I laughed out loud.

Monday night I prayed.
Tuesday morning, another surprise: half toothless, I smiled.

Requiem for a Marriage

I. Invocation

You who know death and Life, be present.
Still our troubled spirits, stir up our joyless hearts.
Our trust dwells in Thee.

II. Confession

Out of the depths I cry,
"Oh, Lord, I tried. Didn't I?"

This emptiness is more raucous than a house
of querulous people, no longer in love, struggling
against the insidious move toward hate—
or worse, apathy—against anger jarring against anger.
Contempt, a canker on the soul of this marriage
ate silently, but with not unhearing ears
did we hear it, feel its vibrations
eroding the foundation.
Struggling in our separateness we protested
against the good we saw, afraid to extol virtue
that might encourage unfaithfulness.
We were, nevertheless, infidels uncommitted
enough, no longer trusting each other or ourselves.

We would not speak the pain of it, nor stir from sloth,
nor face unmet hopes one more time.
We hurled accusations to drown out the quiet,
incessant gnawing of indifference.
Finally, knowing, not knowing, it stopped.
We stopped.

This emptiness rings as loud as death,
echo bounding off bare bones,
no flesh to soften its hollowness,
no spirit giving it even macabre melody:
no pride, no thing inside.

III. Absolution

Little we knew then the knife of truth cuts clean:
a festered wound must not have the whole.
Still good remains.
One gave the gift of laughter, which fed itself,
and one said the other taught compassion,
a growing thing.
Though neither priceless gift could be extended
any longer, we have not lost those treasures.
A new gift—strength—enables us to say
I forgive."
Enhanced, renewed, accepted,
we heal.

The twin burdens, guilt and failure, lighten.
Help comes from nowhere and everywhere,
from now not then, and steps grow quicker, surer.
Godspeed.

IV. Eucharist

We give thanks for possibilities:
a wine-dipped wafer, thanksgiving's bittersweet,
but knowing that Your love is not violable sustains.
While we mend, our trust swells in Thee.

Who Can Know Grief?

Who can this shock assess?
There's quietness, called numbness, no one
should curse or bless.
Who can this loss allay?
No keeper of the lost and found puts emptiness away.
Who can this rage erase?
No one has balm enough to put such anger in its place.
Who can this wild thing tame?
No trainer with a whip and chair could put this fear to shame.
Who can these depths explore?
No matter what we think is known,
tears, like seas, yield more.

Yet persons, wisdom, strength, and health—
Love-stirred—
pour through the funnel of the self,
and grief remains the motive prime
till self becomes a pitcher
to pour back in due, due time.

After Divorce

I never wanted to get married again—it's too complicated,
who were men anyway and what do they want?
(besides the obvious)—
for a few months anyway.

Until I met Jerry, cute, blondish, at Parents Without Partners
(an ersatz dating service), a good dancer at Opus,
then at his house at a PWP discussion meeting.
Later he invited me to another meeting at his house,
saying, somewhat seductively,
"You have to come. It'll be exciting."
Exciting it was not.
It was Amway,
he was trying to get us attendees to become representatives.
He fell in love with Amway—
damn! Amway, shmam-way,
scram-way.

So the hankerin' began.
Next a guy a mutual friend tells me I just have to meet,
also at PWP, insisting we were just right for each other,
looks me over, says, "I thought you'd be younger"
(me that just dyed the gray away!).
His loss, I think.

Then I talk to a swimmate at the "Y," he seeming needy.

He asks to see me, and we go to a movie a night or two later,

first time a man's been in the house since the other left.

Needy wanted to see a scary movie (not my type),

then needed to leave before it ended.

On the second date, he wants to see *The Omen*,

a story of 666's on the forehead, a scary dog,

and other forebodings.

Again, though we sit near the back, he wants to leave early.

But I insist, intrigued by the evil Gregory Peck, and we stick it out.

At home, needy wants to see something on t.v.,

so we go to the basement where his needs become apparent.

Greta, the Weimaraner, has been suspicious all along,

too, and, smelling trouble, noses her way between us.

He being scared of dogs, especially after *The Omen*,

flees, never again to be seen or heard.

Now *I* am scared. Of my judgment, my needs, or are they wants?

Ladies' Troubles

"All women's troubles come from one thing,"
my husband-to-be informs me as we discuss
the terms of our marriage.
"Being ladies and not letting go."

I don't say, that's two things.
"The not letting go part, I know from our grief groups, holding
on to the past, afraid to make a new start . . ."

"No, no, well, that too. But the other more serious,
much more serious thing.
I mean, I've been around enough of you to know
what it is that makes you miserable,
probably causes early death and disease."

I don't ask, in that order?
Somehow I know this is Wisdom speaking.
"Yes?" I prod, when he hesitates.

"You don't know how to let gas."

Nervously and not-so-nervously, I ponder.

"Now take me," he says, offering himself
as an excellent example (I discover later).
"I guess the Marines did it for me, on Guam.
Those that didn't—not many—got sick,
threw up, did their business in the Pacific soon learned"—
"From you?"
"Well, sure, from everyone. Rice and dead animals
and dead bugs and rotten leaves give it to you,
worse than beans,"
and I sure believe him.

"So I won't be offended," he continues.
"I'd rather you did than got sick—
I mean Esther never did learn till her liver
got so sick she couldn't help herself.
It was hard for her to laugh about, her being such a lady . . ."

I realize he's right:
it's such discomfort to be polite.
So, not long after, I practice.
First, in the pool where bubbles jet-propulse
my backstroke back and forth speedily,
especially if beans were in the diet.

Finally one time, silently, I do It near him,
and he announces, his nose twitching, "I'm proud of you."
And that's how I learned to fart, finally.

Bedtime Snack

Warm tea and cinnamon toast, elements as nourishing
as wine and wafer,
we share to consecrate the co-union of our bodies.

The Seconds

He never fails to flirt, outrageously, telling the not-so-pretty girl
or woman, "You're the second-most pretty girl here"
or "You have the second prettiest smile."
When pressed who is the first, he says, "I'll never tell."

He married me, he insists, because the Queen
was not available. I believe it because
whenever I persist in arguing he says,
"Now, Queenie, you know I don't have to win this argument."

We almost saw the Queen once, not closely
enough to argue with her about her governing-style;
besides he'd not have had to win that argument either.
"I'm a lover, not a fighter," he spouts when I still persist,
friendly-like, on my way.
"The only arguments
I need to win are the three percent that matter!"
I find out what they are—really only one—
when he wants to hold me to my half-promise
made on the second night of our acquaintance,
to sell my house and move to an apartment.
The reasonable arguments are on my side
five years later, I think, till he points out how investing
the profit in this strange market will help "the business part"
of our marriage. And how, now that we're traveling more,
we won't have to mow grass, paint, and such.

Still I don't cede till he gives an ultimatum:
sell or I leave.
I hope my son will not later disown me
for what may seem disowning him—
though his being twenty, educated, and with a good job,
it didn't seem that way to me.

So we find a place with year-round swimming
on the premises, a mandatory requirement,
and make the move in September.
Wild-eyed he enters my room where I am teaching
a sixth-grade boy and says, "I lost my keys!"
"But you were to let the movers and utility people in,"
I say so the boy would understand this interruption
and unfolding drama.
I retrieve my keys for him, and he departs.
"My husband has a habit of losing things,"
I say, "but this is the first time he's ever come to school.
I'm sorry he was so frantic."
"I could tell," Andrew says sympathetically,
"and I didn't have the heart to tell him his fly was open."

It is just one of many tales . . .

Our legendary Open House on New Year's Day
features Bavarian kraut, kraut w/sausage
and special seasonings.
Till he is hospitalized for a double hernia surgery,
he lugs the cans home from Ohio.
We search locally and can't find Bavarian-
style in this German community.

But my Mennonite Cookbook answers the need:
use sausage, add dill weed and caraway seed.
The first time we make it ourselves,
guests rave and as we taste it ourselves
with them for the first, he says,
"The reason it's so good is because I doubled the seasonings." I
counter: "I knew you would and only told you half."
The story gets repeated a second, third and fourth time
that day by request and again on following New Years' Days
till, seventeen years later, guests repeat the legend
in his absence, noting he was never second-class
in anything, especially in his and my second marriage.

Counting

I do love you. I will count the why's.

Because I love the sycamore, its textured skin,
its patient, gentle strength and wind-bent height.

Because I love the scented blossom,
intense red or calm clear blue,
fragile flesh bearing fiercely precious beauty.

Because I love the music, the Mozart of your words,
like water whispering, leaping,
like water soothing, dancing,
like water resting, singing, like water cresting,
springing forth from sources dark and deep,
a stream of joy buoying me with life and love and you.

If You Remember

the forties when we were teens,
saving lard, rubber, meat, sugar, paper, nylons,
money, naturally—using stamps for some of the above,
depending on whom you could trade with.

My brother and I filled his Radio Flyer
with newspapers collected from neighbors
and went to Smitty's Junkyard on Dauphin Street
on weekdays to get a better price.
We got a nickel or dime per load,
often hauling ten-twelve loads a morning.
With our nickels we stopped on the way home for Ho-Jo's,
frozen malted milk in chocolate cones.
November through February we went to Smitty's
on Saturday, no matter how cold outside.
For the war effort.

We watched those bombs dropping on our ships
in the Pacific by the dirty Japs,
and energy and determination flared anew.
Lowell Thomas fired our imaginations,
especially as the Ski Patrol in Norway sped down
snowy slopes hunting dirty Krauts.

My husband, seven years older, got his draft notice
and high school diploma on the same day.
The thing he hated most about the military
was that it taught him to hate.
For the yellow vermin to be exterminated—
to bayonet him—you had to see the face of your enemy
as a slanty-eyed monster.
You had to do this to rid *him* from the face
of the earth and to protect your buddy.

On Tinian, he accidentally killed a buddy
on the airfield at night—no headlights on in case
Zeroes dropped their filthy loads on our planes—
when the boy wandered the airfield
to walk off a hang-over
as Keith reconnoitered for spies in a Jeep.
A hearing exonerated him, but guilt remained life-long,
disrupting our sleep in ungodly nightmares
that woke him screaming.

When the Enola Gay left Tinian to drop
its ungodly load on Hiroshima,
many more were sent screaming,
so he didn't think nightmares too big a price for him to pay.

Scenes Seen

—Three pre-teens and teens drumming, fifing,
furling the flag marching oh-so-proudly
down the dusty road
—a 14-year old skipping behind the 60-, 70-year old Yanks
on their way to beat the hell out o' the Rebs—
why, why to join 'em!

—the 12-year old Cuban watching a Maine battleship
blow up in the harbor, lighting the night sky with fury
—the 8-year old in Auvers, blistered and battered,
spitting and sputtering from mustard in the air
—thousands of 6-, 7-, 8-year olds in Hiroshima,
vaporized in one second
—a naked, napalmed oily, sweaty body runs
screaming down a Saigon street
—a Rwandan's small hands and feet chopped off by Hutus
—a 9-year old grinning proudly, fearfully, as the photographer
shoots his armless body, after a bombing meant for Saddam
—a crowd of 7—to 14-year olds, led by their 14-year old
commander, sling rifles over their small shoulders
in Africa, South America, Indonesia.

Obscenities pass behind my lids while making
my quotidian drive down the county roadway.

Magi

Out of the mouths of babes . . . .

The two-year old says ah-me-mah-moo (hippopatamus)
and hop-dop (helicopter), and we laugh.

The five-year old says celery for salary
when I tell him what I make as church secretary
when the pastor and his wife come for supper.
Also I've told him Pastor John can't smell anymore,
so he says, My mom says you don't smell so good.

The ten-year old asks, Why do they kill people?,
the Ten Commandments having taken hold.

The fifteen-year old: Going to Canada?
Yes, I'll be a draft dodger! I'm not serving in no g.d. war!
I'm not dyin' for nobody in no g.d. helicopter!
We don't belong over there!
Six years later, he says, Mom, I can't believe he's going,
as his best buddy goes, goes to Saigon, goes to Hanoi,
goes to the skies over a once-beautiful land.

The twenty-two, twenty-three, twenty-four year olds
go to church and cry when they hear the letter to Mom:
Mom, please don't worry about me. I'm fine.
I'm doing well—
the Huey is the best thing that ever happened to me.

Living to Eat

Snapper soup—it always sounded so gross—
throwing a live turtle, shell and all, into a pot of boiling water!
The chef then, when the animal was soft enough,
picked the meat from the shell, glac`ed the broth,
finally served it with a cruet of sherry.

Keith urged me to try it, just a taste first from his,
then to order my own cup.
Lobster, too, ends up being boiled alive.
I never tried *it* either—too expensive
and how do you pick the darn meat from the claws?
But Keith said to try it, ordering one for both of us.
He cracked the claw with the little hammer, used the pick
to stab the meat, told me to dip it in butter, and—
Did I just die and go to heaven?

A Fine Restaurant/
Ristorante/Restaurante

Gourmandy gourmets ingest gustatory greats into grateful gullets
on smooth and slick and shiny linens, china, silver.
Silver and glass chandeliers sparkle,
and gleam on bright mirrors images plates and trays
groaning with gravies and grapes and glasses and greatness.

Tinkling pianos and troubadours traipsing
around tables pleasure couples pleasing each other
on a fine evening out, prelude to more and more and more.

Gentle laughter wafts to the mirrored ceiling,
floats to the soft, deep Aubisson below
where footfalls impress their mark.

Coolness, soft scents, tall menus from tuxedoed men and women
with red bow ties tied perfectly straight.

Later taxis await for this night on the town to end,
to wend through deserted streets under mild blinking lampposts,
no horns to interrupt the fantasy.

The diners, sated and tired, put their wallets away
and slip between silky smooth cool sheets.

Drivers and waiters, sweepers and polishers go home too,
to children and wives waiting and slip between cotton percale,
pull soft woolen blankets up and over and lay their heads
on downy pillows—satisfied with one night's fine work.

Hotels and "Hotels"

My husband believes you get more local flavor if you avoid
four-star places and secure a place in the residents' quarters
when on foreign soil.

Foreign soil is what you sometimes get.
For instance, in London during their semi-sescentennial,
when rooms were hard to arrange for in advance,
he consults Fodor and asks me to get a room months ahead.

"Lovely rooms in the such-and-such district"
(I'm not sure now what district it was,
only some "foreign quarters,") Fodor announces.
The brochure-on-the-phone announces "Best rooms available,
especially during the semi-sescentennial.
We've had people booking ten years in advance."

"Home-style cooking available. Close to subway stop."
Since we always do a lot of hoofing, that last was the biggest draw.

We arrived about two p.m., two blocks from the Tube stop,
noting the pleasant street with its colorful old row house fronts,
a few old trees, some small gardens, the flavor of England, to be
sure.

We found the address with ease, a good sign
in case Tracy and I get separated from her grandfather,
ring some crazy kind of doorbell
(doorbells being as varied in Europe as the way you flush toilets),
and a man in a turban answers.
"Yes?" "We have rented a room," Keith says, perhaps redundantly.
Are there other reasons people ring these doorbells?
(A resounding yes, we learn later, a redolent yes.)
The room is on the second floor, no problem, even though there is,
understandably in a centuries-old flat, no elevator.
A narrow and dark stairway warns: how do we evacuate in case of fire?
The room, too, is dark
with one high window on a far wall with one single bed.
"We are three," Keith explains, again somewhat redundantly,
although, truthfully, in the dimness, the turbaned figure
may have difficulty discerning.

The smell—what is it? I wonder—later identifying curry wafting
from a kitchen in the nether regions,
confirming the identity of the turban-wearer.
Soon another smell, sweeter, wafts. Curry and pot!
Not curry *in* the pot. Curry *and* pot.
"This won't do," Keith says, looking needlessly at me.
"We are three. We need at least two beds, preferably doubles."
"Can do," Turban says. We leave, somewhat satisfied our wishes
will be met. On returning a few hours later,
long enough for him to find something suitable
(and after Tracy says, "I just know there's bugs!"
(thoughts *I* daren't express to confirm her hypochondriac nature),
we are shown our new room, this one outfitted with a window twice
the size of the former, next door to the former.
The bathroom is in the same "complex,"
a great feature for the three of us,
all of us subject to two a.m. calls.
It looks no cleaner, and somewhat to my horror,
Keith who doesn't look at us this time, says, "We'll take it."
The double bed, the *one* double bed, fills the room completely.
"I just know there's bugs," Tracy says.
And one of us—who is so brave as to lie at 8 p.m.,
exhausted and hungry—says, "Of course not, honey.
Didn't you smell the fumigation?"
(How would you have been able to tell, mixed with curry and pot?)

"Do you know where we can get a bite to eat?" Keith asks,
one who usually explores for emporiums. Turban frowns.
"We close kitchen at 6 p.m., open at 6 a.m."
Great! Curry and pot and fumigation to be our alarm clock.
Nearby we find a cute little place offering Indian(!) cuisine
and just about to close, but the proprietor, summoned by a lean waiter,
surveys our emaciated conditions, decides to serve us when we say
we're staying just down the street.
The food is passable, and I who never liked curry take a few bites
just to stave the pangs for a few hours.

When we return to our abode for the next five nights
(Keith always theorizes that we only need a place for sleeping
anyway), we push the bed against the wall, just in case one of us
needs room to escape to the bathroom at two a.m.

"I'm not sleeping against the wall," Tracy reasons, rather vehemently,
given how tired she must be after sixteen to twenty hours of
wakefulness, miles of sight-seeing in a less seedy London,
and starvation. We nod knowingly.
"We know, we know, just in case there's bugs."

So in this settling-in phase of our odyssey,
who will sleep against the wall?
When younger than these thirteen years,
she slept between us on trips, so she wouldn't fall out of bed,
to pull on Grampa's beard to wake him up, to announce,
always with alarm, "Grampa, take me to the bathroom!"

Keith, in his fifties, had developed the habit of running to pee
many times a night, so it was determined he should sleep
on the outside, only a few feet from the bathroom door.
Me being the smaller of the three could more easily crawl
over the other two at two a.m.
We were so tired, we dropped off immediately, with our clothes on.

Guess what? I saw nothing crawling on the wall all night long—
truly, amazingly, there were "no bugs."

Bruges, 1992

The last city in Europe we visit—after three-and-a-half weeks
of Paris, Nantes, Angers, Paris again, Honfleur, Etretat, Auvers, and
Paris,
Braunschweig, Hamelin, Hannover, Kassel (for the best in the
world Rembrandts), Wittenberg, Brussels—is Bruges, Venice of the
North, with its canals and stunning pre-Renaissance-era architecture
intact.

The Belgians are a sturdy lot. Keith is not, his belly swelling
the first week in Paris even *before* three days of plumbing gone
awry.
When Ursula asks, after visiting several of their cities,
where we would like to go next, he says, "Could we just stay
home?"
A leisurely morning of Klaus's grilled sausage and Ursula's fluffy
eggs, rest, talk, and laughter does much to heal.
Then an afternoon trip to the local bookstore for yet other art books,
with me insisting we ship *these* home.

Reluctantly we bid our first Friendship Force friends from 1980
good-bye and board a night train bound for Brussels.
A Dutch-speaking conductor wakes us at seven, in time to freshen
and take a city bus tour—Keith usually abhors these
for the time they waste stopping at gift shops,
but we locate our priorities and return to them later:
a lace-making factory and art museum where Keith
revels in his favorite school, the Flemish.
From the large, bustling, efficient train station we leave Brussels
and take such a delightful journey through the countryside,
we know we've done the right, refreshing thing
by ending our journey at Bruges.
In this small walkable town we find a brand-new Novatel,
unpack and rest. On a smackingly sunny morning we explore.
First discovery: a Pieta by Michelangelo!
surely the label is wrong in the dimly lit chapel
at The Church of Our Lady.
Since photography's not permitted, I buy *Bruges on Foot*
and sure enough, the picture and description confirm
this is probably the first of Buenorrati's Madonna and Child's
this with its out-of-proportion babe—
not an adult Christ removed from the cross—
standing in front of Mary between her knees.
Most assuredly Michelangelo intended for the Babe to be so large
to emphasize His importance over His mother and foreshadow
His untimely demise.

Breathless from this discovery, we move to others, equally stunning:
Keith sits (and perhaps is momentarily restored)
contemplating Roger van der Weyden's *The Rapture*
at the Groening, a strange collection of masterpiece paintings,
antique cooking tools quaintly arrayed on the walls.

Each afternoon we return to our lovely room at the Novatel,
rest and cuddle, and—thus reinforced—visit another museum
before a "night on the town."
And what nights they were!
Street singers and players of many varieties.
Stunning night-lit city buildings on the large cobble-stoned square.
June scents of kaleidoscope-filled window boxes, arbors, canopies
mix with the foods we choose in an abundance of restaurants.

The trip to Ghent almost fails. Arriving at noon, we learn the
cathedral is hosting a wedding—no visitors allowed.
We wait nearby on a bench, sharing a dripping waffle,
when we see bustle. The party emerges and with a few other
lucky tourists we approach the caretaker.

Oh-but-you-see-the-crypt then perhaps the triptych.
We do not need to see more bones and stains of bloodied martyrs,
but to see Van Eyck, we comply.
The caretaker leads us to a darkened side chapel.
With much ceremony he turns on special lighting,
removes protective shields,
and the *Adoration of the Mystic Lamb* unfolds,
after the anunciatory angels, saints, and gospel-writers,
to reveal a tiny Lamb standing on a red box
at the bottom of the center panel, surrounded
by more worshipping angels and pre-Renaissance people,
patrons surely included.
Above the Lamb panel is the seated, bearded Messiah,
triple-crowned, with scepter, His right hand raised in blessing,
a larger, more intricate crown at the hem of His scarlet robes.
A crowned Virgin is on the right
and an unadorned Joseph on his Son's left.
Outer panels show the naked Adam and Eve,
white horses, and more townspeople.
We had studied iconography but the symbolism
here is so complicated, beautiful, and mysterious,
we cannot begin to comprehend it.

We and others wish to be allowed to see the rear panel
as it is most unusual to find the center back panel painted,
for no worshipers are allowed there, just the priests.
We tell the caretaker who is taking much too much care,
we believe, We have traveled far, from the U. S., sir—
he's not impressed—from New York, sir, from California, sir,—
he's not impressed—from Pennsylvania, sir. Please?
His eyes light up. Did the "please" do it?
The lovely sound of "Pennsylvania"?
Does he have a nephew in the priesthood in Philadelphia?
He nods. But first, he says—he hesitates—
there is a box, a box to protect the masterpiece.
He points to the sign in various languages above it:
Please donate to protect *The Adoration of the Lamb*.
A little chart suggests so many francs, so many marks,
so many dollars (five) are suggested.
Keith digs in his money belt, retrieves all but a very few marks
and drops them in, forty or fifty dollars.
Then we are led to the back. More lights are switched on
as the ones in front are extinguished.

At this writing, the best I can recall
(my mind still reeling at the overwhelming beauty and symbolism)
is we saw Mystery Itself:
a rather uncomplicated smallish Cross of Calvary
with the suffering Lord, but above it is the triumphal glorious
figure of Christ ascending into heaven,
His Father waiting to receive Him.
Such whiteness.

Of the many reasons Keith wanted to visit this treasure
is that its colors and detail are so marvelously preserved.
It has never been restored in five-and-a-half centuries,
yet it's so brilliant you almost don't need external lighting.
And it is the tallest triptych in the world,
the center panel some fourteen-to-sixteen feet.
Sint Baafs-Kathedraal's chapel ceiling is high enough for it;
indeed, the church-patron who commissioned the painting
built the *kathedraal* to accommodate it in 1432.

Keith, by the last evening, can eat hardly anything,
yet samples, and miraculously, keeps things down.
We had ridden the canal boat, visited the Hopital
(hospital-turned-museum), bought a lace collar
where they took our last marks for film also.
Keith, having foresworn Belgian chocolate, the best in the world,
says, "Buy the film."
I gave the smiling proprietor our last lucre.
Happily, she seemed to like Americans.

Walk and sit, rest, eat. On the last of four afternoons,
we visit gift shops along another canal, and thanks to Visa,
are able to buy a 3x3 ceramic plaque of a brown, red, white, and
grey canal with a hovering burnt-red tile roof.

Viewing all that Flemish majestic awe
had been a sort of prayer for Keith and me
(perhaps that's why the Flemish seemed to draw him):
The van Eyck, van Der Wyden's *Rapture*
with hundreds being assumed to their final joy,
in greys and blues and more triumphal white.

In Bruges my prayers had become more explicit:
I bargained Just let me get him home alive,
Lord, alive, and we'll never travel again.

We leave a busy Brussels airport and land in a busy Philadelphia
airport, Keith so worn, ill, and obese, he can barely handle luggage.
We're penniless, but a perfect stranger pays for a wheeled luggage
cart,
pitying perhaps, perhaps obeying the prayer to get him home alive.
Worst is the commuter's delay of several hours,
making us arrive home at eleven p.m. instead of seven.

Danke schoen. You did it. *Danke schoen,*
all of you. Whenever I'd objected to spending money to go
overseas, Keith would matter-of-factly say We're buying memories.
Now, thanks to Kodak, to our hosts in France, Germany,
Belgium, Philadelphia, we have memories of Bruges.
In March 1995, weeks before he goes to his rapture,
we affirm that Bruges was the best,
the absolute best trip of all. All of it,
even the illness, in spite of the illness.

Danke schoen, Gott.

To Keith

Walking hand-in-hand, we said,
heart-to-heart, head-to-head,
we build mem'ries to grow old on:
grapefruit, ballet, baseball, art—
until death do us part—
these are anchors we can hold on.

But that will not be the end,
father, brother, lover, friend,
I know there is another door:
explore, explore, discover more.

Sixtieth Birthday

As usual, Deb, Tom, Keith, and I celebrate together,
this time over weinerschnitzel, steak, pork chop, sole.

There's a sweet card, and Tom says,
"I don't know anyone younger than you.
I don't mean just in looks, I mean in the way you think."

I open their gifts: gold circlets for my ears,
scented candle and shower gel, and chocolate, always chocolate.
After we share desserts, Deb and I pack the presents
in the pink flowered bag.
But, really, who needs gifts when your son,
this son who calls you every week if you don't call him first,
has already bestowed the best.

Eulogy to Our Step-Dad, 1995

We loved you because you never gave advice unless we asked.
Then, typically, it was laced with experience, wisdom, humor.

We loved it when you became friends with our father,
a rare thing indeed.

You had many fine qualities, but the one we admire and treasure
most and will remember forever is integrity.

Maples

The dried winged samaras, dried seeds within,
crowd the early October sidewalks,
late-droppers who sank rather than
propellered their way down in spring,
some landing on the railroad-tie wall
where I frequently rest on a daily walk.
They're not graceful or pretty anymore as
their brothers and sisters in April were, ugly even.
Yet life burgeons within, a century or more of shade
to shelter—another reason I stop to rest on the wall
holding back the lawn from the maple's sturdy roots
trying to burst out and crack the concrete.

My own maple barely survives after twenty-two years
of being over-shadowed by my neighbor's Bradford pear,
planted too closely.
Two arborists said to get rid of one or we'd lose both.
One said the maple should go, as it had four things
wrong with it: split bark into which thingies
had been nesting and burrowing to the pulp,
roots pushing above the grass,
more-than-normal moss on all sides,
not just the north, and others which have
surely escalated by now.

When Hurricane Hannah brought two large
rotted pear limbs crashing onto my property
this September causing much damage
(Act of God, says insurance, so I'm responsible.
If He/She can act to destroy,
why can't She/He pay my repairs too?
But it doesn't work that way,
not to my chagrin because I'm alive,
having missed the accident by a few minutes).

In October when other maples
blaze orange, red, yellow, burnished salmon,
up and down the street, mine lags.
Yet near month's end, it will offer its palette
and announce its longevity,
before it turns its skeleton limbs upwards to winter.

Spring Daffodils, I

Mother teaches me, at age five,
to plant daffodils in October in honor of my birth month, April,
when they bloom.

At school in first grade Miss Buller reads a poem about daffodils
and teaches us how to make paper ones to put in our May
baskets.
Cut and make a cylinder of yellow paper, fringe one end
and cut slits in the other, making the "steeple,"
cut a circle of yellow, make "triangle" cuts on the outer edge
and glue the cylinder onto it.
A long green stem and two slender leaves complete this beauty.

It was hard to put it into my May basket since we were
"obligated" to deliver our May basket to our special love on
May first.
Since I loved the daffodil, I wasn't sure who to deliver it to.
Daffodils graced every garden I ever rented or owned in April.

When I first attended college at age thirty-three,
my composition professor assigned *The Glass Menagerie*.
We were to pick a character and develop an essay on him or her.
Amanda and her nine mentions of jonquils had to be mine.
(Why so many jonquils in a tiny flat?)
The O.E.D. helped: jonquils were a member
of the narcissus family, as is the daffodil, and piteable as she is,
Amanda is certainly narcissistic.
Professor Charles suggested I read my essay to the class as a
good example of essay writing. I said the O.E.D. was
responsible
and have been explaining daffodils ever since.

My daughter-in-law started bringing daffodils
every spring after our Tom died.
By now I'd learned to dismiss their musky scent
and appreciate her loving remembrance.

Late October I met my love and learned he lost his wife
to cancer after twenty-six years
as I'd lost my spouse to divorce after twenty-five.
The first evening I asked more about Esther's passing
and learned their (and my) favorite movie was *Dr. Zhivago*
because of the scene where the survivors
of that horrid winter of starvation and revolution stumble over
a snowy hill to fields of daffodils beckoning new life.

One evening Esther told Keith to get something to eat.
When he returned, the nurse said Esther had died in his absence,
but asked her to tell Keith to "remember the daffodils."
As he relates this tale to me, the tears roll and I decide
right then and there I would marry him if he asked me
because any man who was not afraid to show
such vulnerability, would make a good mate.
We choose a diamond daffodil surrounded
by green emerald leaves for the engagement ring.

Fifteen years later, as I emerge from Tudor Castle,
I am surprised by "clouds of daffodils" as far as the eye can see.
I see Keith sitting in the midst of them, weeping.
"I'm sorry," he says.
"It's okay, Keith."
"I'm sorry," he apologizes again.
"It's okay, Keith, it's beautiful . . .
seventeen years is a beautifully long time."

Three years later he is gone. I have not only lovely memories to
sustain me but lovely art that we purchased together.
There's been no need to add to that until—until!
I see *Spring Daffodils* and know instantly I must have it,
the only impulse purchase I've ever made in my life.
The local artist visits my house when I ask her advice on where
to hang it and also to see the art Keith and I have collected.

Now, winter and summer I will have daffodils
to weather me through 'most anything.
I can touch the thick paint of those "steeples"
and think of Esther and Keith and Mother . . . and Miss Buller.

Meals-on-Wheels

I learn so much from my clients, their sturdiness
and humor informing my old age.
Impressive is the sweet way husbands tend ailing spouses.
We don't get many the other way around
because healthy wives can still cook.

Lucky me, enabling them to stay in their homes
because of the service a while longer—some for five years or more.

I always tell them, "It's a really good meal today."
I know it is, 'cause I needed the service too,
and 'cause anticipation is the appetite stimulant many need.

I ask how they are and listen to a litany of complaints
I willingly forbear so I may offer a word of encouragement and
empathy—and learn something about resilience.
Some just need the contact as they see no one else
but their Meals-on-Wheels visitor from day to day.

You never know what you'll find.
Many people leave the door unlocked, expecting you
to walk in and call their name.
If they don't respond, I walk throughout the home or apartment
to make sure they're "safe and sound"
(sometimes they're not), leave the meal.

Once, after trying to locate where the meal was to be
left for a brand-new client, I put it at a side door.
Two days later, scanning the obituaries, I saw the man's name.
He died the morning I we tried to make that delivery,
a good reason for not opening the door!
Another time, I find our client on the floor beside his bed.
I ascertain he's not bleeding, is breathing okay,
and has not broken any bones.
I get my driver, and together we help get him into his chair.
We talk with him to make sure he's really okay,
and he says, "I'll eat later."
To our concern he says, "I'm a tough old bird."
He is, having farmed all his life and still lives on the homestead.
The following week, following my suggestion,
he's wearing Life-Alert.

When I ask, another client says his cat has no name,
but he calls him "Mom."
"How many litters has she had?" I ask.
And he says, "None. It's a boy."
All in a day's work.

285-7305: Car Trouble!

Rescue? Who? Who else?
My fifth call in as many weeks. This time for brakes.
Joe's a good guy, son Mike too, and wife Barb's a peach
—she brings me home when I don't want to wait,
who knows? how long? Sometimes Joe has a pretty good guess,
others its hit-or-miss.
Sometimes he can't take me at all; once last month I had
to wait a whole week.
I got cabin fever.

Why are we so dependent on these infernal combustion engines?
You'd think we're *they're* servants.
The Bonneville—my Bonnie—has been so reliable for fourteen
years I can't believe she needs so much care recently.
Hang in there, kiddo. I'd like to keep you for my lifetime:
ten? twenty? years to go?

Mid—and Low-Technology

High technology—things with buttons, dials, switches
that confound more than work as intended—is over-rated.

Give me mid-technology: potato peelers, garlic presses.
pizza cutters, old-fashioned cheese slicers
and low—needle and thread, knives, forks, spoons,
pens and pencils.

Please, inventors:
give me these that don't blow my mind.
Like the lowly hammer and scissors.

Touching Paper

Imagine a world paperless.
Polyethylene chloride combinants, stiff, sticking, stifling
when wrapping or microfilming, which, in spite of transparency
are too tough to be vulnerable, and cathodes, transistors,
capacitors,
obfuscating with their circuitry,
assaulting ears and eyes with tree-of-knowledge arrogance
too often without time-healing wisdom or humility
(except when their life-switch is activated to off),
try to make paper antecedant.

Imagine a world where paper is no longer smooth and cool
as a windowpane, rough as sand scraping the sole, thick as a flax
leaf,
thin as a moth wing, fluttery as the wind or a flower petal,
where the pulp of its parent is no longer wetted, rolled, and
pressed,
its ridges fitting fingerprint whorls.

Imagine a world where words can be seen (polyethelene)
and heard (the electronic word)
but not felt.
Though fragile, paper can, like the mind, be imprinted
with more than alphabets.

No, cathodes, transistors, capacitors—electronics—
cannot replace print or phonics.
Polyethelene chloride combinants—vinyl—
though non-biodegradable are not final.
Paper—the heart of a tree recording textured memory—
is a leaf of eternity.

Answering Machine

The robot voice announces, "You have an appointment
on Friday at 2:14."
It's good she called. I thought it was 2:15.

I never fail to check as soon as I'm in the house—and do the
follow-up, for once, it said I'd better come fast, our Tom may be
dead! dead!
though the news is dispatched in doses
(one doesn't tell such stories all at once).

And another time it told that our Scott was being rushed
to Hershey Med Center for emergency removal of his colon,
which had perforated days before, and before that, his lung
and maybe heart had been punctured by the cycle falling on him
when he jumped the hill the third time
(the first two being successful—he's not *that* reckless!)
And another announced his eight-year cocaine use and abuse,
though now he'd gone cold turkey for more than a year,
a cherished Mother's Day tale, a secret revelation,
its honesty binding us together,

and another on New Year's Day: "Mom, I asked Denise
to marry me last night!"
I didn't have to ask her answer from the joy on the line.

So, yes, I always check the answering machine.
It may detail yet another thread of life, connecting
to trivia and life and Being.

Prayer

"Oh, God!" is what you say in distress,
not for some picayunish thing like a flat tire
or "laughing" at a flat joke,
when your pencil point breaks in the middle of a note,
when you mistake "define" for "divine"
and you think you're going blind.

No-no-no!

It's what you say when you get the divorce papers,
when the undertaker calls to say it's impossible to cremate your
wife's remains, when your child is found dead.

And you don't say "Oh, God."
You say, "Oh, my God."

Disaster

Too many—a hundred every week—airliner or helicopter crashes,
kidnappings, murders, rapes assault the senses
till I turn off t.v.—"compassion fatigue" it's called.

"Dis" (away from) and "aster" (star) is the old notion
Shakespeare used a lot that the stars are not favorable to us.

Onstar saves us from the disaster of getting lost
or not being found if we wreck the car.
But it cannot save from losing a child—whether soon or late,
no matter what the cause of separation—
or from losing your heart.

Road Kill

He swerved to avoid the rabbit, squirrel, but ran over it anyway.
It was already dead, and he thought, You can only die once.
Not true!
You die more than once, a thousand times, when the doctor
says your wife's lump was not benign,
and too bad your father does not have brain cancer,
for then I could remove the offensive thing
robbing his memory and I can't operate because your mother's
small arteries are so clogged, too, it won't help to by-pass
the large ones and your four-year old grand-child does
not have ADD, it's leukemia and you can't afford
to put your wife into a good nursing home
and your second grandchild is born blind
and everybody's heart is breaking
nine hundred and ninety-nine times.

Rain

The rain beats against the windowpane
with the wings of a frightened cardinal.
It runs down the glass in frantic pathways,
spreading out like jagged feathers
and settles limply on the windowsill.

For the Arthritic

Rain =pain. Complain!
Prayin', prayin, prayin . . .
Gain!
Explain?
Prayin', prayin', prayin' . . . .

Going to Funerals

Did you ever have a car fright and wonder
who would come to your funeral?
Would it be the little girl who needed a ride in the rain,
the harried housewife who ran out of gas on a main
highway,
the hitchhiker on his way to the meth clinic and was
running late,
the thin grandmother who overturned her ankle
on the way to market whom you passed by,
speeding to somewhere unimportant?

With God in the passenger seat we think of the least of these,
and, like Lazarus, hope we can tell others before it's too late.

Obits.

They used to be free; now they charge so much per line,
not inch, mind you, to tell the world you expired
on so-and-so day at such-and-such place
sometimes also for this-or-that reason.
Relatives, hobbies, careers—it all adds up.
You'd think at least they'd spell your name right.

Steeping

I take my tea bag out in thirty seconds
while my Chinese student Kai lets his in for three to five
minutes,
relenting only when he wants to drink,
Zhang liking tang with his lesson.
When I discover green tea, he smiles: "Ah, Teacher, the best."
Then green tea with mango, with peach
(we look up the fruits in the dictionary) but blueberry?
He frowns and tastes. "Aah. Just don't steep too long, Teacher."

When this thirty-nine year old complains that the lessons
are too hard and it's taking too long, four years so far,
to learn English—"I just a baby," he says, meaning he's made
no progress—I say, having fortuitously heard this on television,
"Kai, it can take at least ten years to become fluent."

He studies me. Then he says (his lesson, his gift to me),
"I sure hope Teacher long life."

Complaint #1,000, and Prayer

Arthur-itis, migranes, ulcers—which part of my body
needs the most attention today?

Noxious smells (Diesel among them), too much/too little
rainfall,
too much/too little sunshine, it's too expensive, we're too poor.

Those people overseas (and here) with polluted, shrunken
bodies,
out of sight and sound and smell, we think,
but, thanks to modern technology, not out-of-heart.

There must be something we can do besides giving money.
Lord, how do we give ourselves?

A Conversation with Pain

Hello old friend. I did not invite you,
but now that you're here, you may come in a little while.

I'll look at your wares:
textbooks puzzles maps & other miscellany.
Say that last time you were here you left a piece of yourself
behind.
I was just going to mind it till your next visit
but somehow it became a part of me in spite of myself
and now—I'm sorry—but I can't give it back.
You wouldn't want it: it's no longer you, but me inside
with all the other merchandise I've bought elsewhere.

Thank you for it anyhow. You have plenty to go around,
you say? Don't I know it!

Just leave anything if you think really I need it.
I'm sure it'll come in handy when I least expect it.
Wait! You didn't let me pay you.
Here's a pair of slippers to help you tread softly wherever next
you go.

Courage, Stubbornness, Tenacity

"You have such courage," my friend said,
noting perseverance through illness.
"What choice do I have if I don't want to become an invalid?"

Courage is what the Wright Brothers had at Kitty Hawk,
what an astronaut has every time he steps into a space craft,
what a surgeon prays for every time she opens a skull,
what parents have when they bring a child into the world,
and what fuels the ninety-two year-old every blessed day.

Loneliness

You know you're a widow when there's no one to—
    —tell you your slip is hanging out before you leave the house
    —hold your place in line at the supermarket
    —guard the Men's Room door so you can go
when the Ladies Room is full.

You know you're a widow when—
    —the bills come for you, the Ms.,
rather than "Mr. and Mrs."
    —you begin to understand the freedom
the automobile gives (to cry and to go)
    —and you can fantasize guilt-free
about the gorgeous guy at the gas station.

Dating While Lonely

It is still not lawful in any state
to shoot married couples for holding hands.
My romantic notions seem to have fled:
a harvest moon only inspires thoughts
of a wrinkled orange, and a new moon
only makes me think of a toe-nail clipping.

Soon, however, I may find joy in
sexy imaginings about that handsome
fellow at the bank, for instance.

If you date younger men, you may feel flattered
by the wisdom you've suddenly acquired.
On the other hand, counseling and band-aiding hurts
may become the central focus of your time together.

Dating older men has distinct advantages.
First and foremost, they think of you as positively *young*
(no matter what your age).
On the other hand, there looms the prospect
of cataracts and hearing aids.
blood pressure pills and pacemakers,
doctor visits and medication reminders,
prostate treatments and, well, you get the picture.

Decisions, Decisions

You will probably realize that being a widow is not all bad the first
time you don't have to ask, "What do you want to eat?"
Or you don't get cold-shocked by ceramic because
he forgot to lower the seat.
But any elation at finding yourself Lordess of the Manor
is somewhat offset by the sickening feeling in the pit of the stomach
that now all the decisions are yours.

Memorabilia

Don't throw things out hastily.
You may need your husband's pajama top to sleep with at night,
for the scent, your adult son's long-outgrown teddy bear,
worn fuzz and all, after he is gone, for the scent,
your wife's closetful of dresses for dances and birthday celebrations,
redolent of Arpege No. 5, the pictures—oh, the pictures—
turn them to the wall for as long as the hurt is hot.
Then miraculously, memories will sweeten,
their scent healing you and perhaps others.

Tabloids

Some Stories Really Are TRUE!!!
The politician's, often, the movie star's, likely,
the wife-beater's, natch.

The Bible's a tabloid, too:
John the Baptist's head on a platter (gross!),
Salome dancing with the seven veils,
Sarai getting pregnant at age 100—Abe even older,
Israelites getting out of Egypt
and going to the Promised Land.
(It really, really *did* take forty years,
try as hard as Moses might.)

Good News travels fast—
bad even faster, everyone knows.
Everyone knows where to find the tabloids:
on their own bookshelf!!!

Touch

We need it, you know, all of us, not just babies
(they die without it),
old people (they die better with it),
but all of us, especially the grieving.
We, all of us, need outright, down-right,
honest-to-goodness bear hugs,
as good as kisses sometimes,
to make the blood flow and the heart beat.
They're best when given freely,
when someone's story or sickness or heart touches us.
A hand on the shoulder or arm,
or a hand taking a hand
can send hope to a hurting soul.

Good-Bye, Tom

We've already said good-bye to your smile,
that sparkle in your eye and infectious laugh,
good-bye to the sound of your voice,
your words of encouragement,
to hugs, gentle and warm.

We've already said good-bye to the belief
that we'd have you forever.

We've said hello to memories
more precious than the heart can bear
of honesty, wit, and compassion,
of struggle and pain,
determination, acceptance,
courage and sacrifice,
and the sweet joy of your music,

Hello to pain born from love whose size
we never knew.

We'll never say good-bye to memories
but today we bid farewell to what's left,
ashes to ashes, dust to dust,
good-bye to questions without answers,
grateful you've found peace in a home
more lovely than any we've yet shared.

We say good-bye today only because
someday, once more,
we'll say hello.

Sister Rose

Sister Rose of the Adorers of the Precious Blood
of Jesus and I meet at a Jesuit Retreat, taking a
workshop on the "hard" emotions: fear, anger, grief, guilt.

When I confess my fear of Alzheimer's,
she exudes concern my way, and at lunch I learn
she's Director of Pastoral Care at a nursing facility nearby,
so we vow to keep meeting periodically.

Anger is not the problem for me that it is for the men
their having been told to be "strong" and "men" long
before they are men.

Grief, another story. I don't deal with it much better than fear,
the double deaths of lover and son a year apart
having made me want to give up,
but I know Rose'll be there for me.

Guilt, the "hardest" of all, embracing, as it does, the others
and tending to cling—causing more clinging by the clingee to it,
an evil, vicious cycle,
as though that improves your health, is last.

Brother Paul suggests, for our quiet time,
the passage on the road to Emmaus and reflect
as we did for the other "hards," then write.
When we meet for sharing time, he doesn't ask us to share,
unless we really want to, in his wisdom.
"Bring your slips of paper—just condensations—"
he says eyeing the reams some have written,
"to the covered walkway beside the garden
at four o'clock, near the grill."
My "reams" are heavy—loaded with a parent's years'
worth of pain, made more acute recently,
from "Why was I so harsh?" and "Why did I tell him
[in my sudden happiness] that I may move away?"
when I knew in my bones, he'd probably never
heal from that shock he received eight months before
from the transformer, when I knew how devastating
fear of death could be, almost as devastating
as fear of never getting back to work
or losing your wife because of all this.
Then I no longer feared death, wished it would
come, peacefully, as his had done.

I'm not sure I want to share outdoors
even in that beautiful lilac-scented garden
with the Virgin's statue lovingly embracing all in her presence.
But curiosity—perhaps an important "soft" emotion—
and surely a sense of mystery drive me.
At 3:50 I am there, along with everyone else.

No one speaks. A few nervous twitters when we wonder
if Brother Paul is late. Soon he appears, matchbox in hand.
his solemnity matching ours.
Who will speak first, I wonder. Not I, who spoke first of fear.
Quiet continues to descend.
Then Brother Paul prays a short prayer,
and says we should place our guilts into the bowl.

One by one, not looking at each other, we follow his order,
and he strikes the match. At first the fire does not catch
and someone nervously implores God to "send us a little hell."
God listens, knowing we've all been in hell too, too long.
And the flame catches.
We watch as wisps of smoke ascend,
burning paper stings our nostrils,
our souls scorched duly, our souls ascend
with each small lick of flame.
We watch, mesmerized, the forgiveness almost immediate,
the forgiveness promised in our Eucharists and baptisms,
our tears the only water we need to be clean now,
till the flames slowly die, die, die,
as do our collective guilts in a barbecue grill
at a Jesuit Center in Wernersville, Pennsylvania.

Textures

Not only linen and cotton, silk and challis, voile and chiffon,
brocade and damask, velvet, wool, and pique,
but skin—a baby's, your own!—a rose's, and powder,
silky and light talc between, around and under the toes,
fur of the dog or cat, feathers, carpets, blankets,
curtains, window panes, the feel of ozone before and after rain,
a sneeze, a tickle, mashed potatoes or ice cream
when they squiggle between your teeth
or slide smoothly down your throat, a coin in your pocket.
Our finger whorls are delighted and we smile,
the neatest feeling of all.

Magnetic Resonance Imaginer

Unsyncopated buzzes, clicks, clacks, pulsations, vibrations
measure thewy sinews, veinous' traps for corpuscles
and platelets, marrow for the morrow, neurons escaping,
heartbeats accelerating, through wires and tubes, atoms
tumbling.

Fear melts away: in that altered state the love tunnel talks,
not whispering certainly,
just teasings of creation exploring Creation.

Nuclear magnetites resonate—attract/repel, attract/repel—
in synapses of their own as silences re-arrange
for different slices while breathing goes on as the dye is cast.
Layers, intact, yield.
Far from occult, though mystifying, God speaks, films,
de-codes plane by plane, to show where nature's stumbling.

Fearfully and Wondrously Made

Bones break and heal, muscles, tendons, ligaments
are prayed over.
Systems: digestive, skeletal, endocrine, circulatory, respiratory,
nervous—all "love systems"—ply their trade, separately it
seems,
sometimes aided by palliatives (pain warning when trouble
bodes),
yet all are marvelously connected.

Now hear the word of the Lord.

Leaves

The leaves on the sidewalk are dry and wrinkled,
pale, pale yellow, dark brown, dark maroon
as an old blood stain.
Still I don't like to tread on them.

Ah, there's a green one lying, not too wrinkled yet,
languid, placid.

Maybe in the mid-November of my life I've still
moisture inside, the juice to keep life flowing
a few more years, endorphins sparking.

October Walk

We go for the untouched pungency before man-touched acridity
and for the red/brown/orange/yellow riot
scuffling over our shoes and a few stray birds
who haven't yet heard a swan song.

We go above the shiny Susquehanna to the woods
in Sam Lewis' Park in York County
where after parking we go down the hill
then up through pines to the sturdy October maples, birches,
beeches, elms—of course we go to the oaks whose acorns
squirrels scamper and dig through mounds of leaves for.

This day, a bright windy Saturday morning, there are kites!
soaring up and down the hill over the river
catching up-drafts and down-drafts.
Parents, couples, seven-year olds and thirteen-year olds
joyously competing to see who can fly highest,
who can knock the other's out, whose is largest,
smallest, fastest, prettiest—
some will enter contests later so this is a dry-windy run.
Unbelievably fast clouds try to knock competitors down.
Some strings get broken, get repaired, tears are wiped.
We can hardly abandon our walk,
but are mesmerized by this unexpected glory,
the beautiful laughter and tears of parents and children
and onlookers.

The pungency calls, so we answer and do our trudging,
not realizing we will only do this one time more.
After that we will only reminisce every October
of the walk that restores sanity, up and down the hills,
past shiny green laurel with dried-up blooms still clinging.

The Age Effect: Exaggeration

Seems like some things grows stronger as you get older,
like Grampa's spit overshootin' the spitoon even with practice,
'n' spite'n Gramma's tellin' him to quit.
Like Bronco gettin' meaner 'n' meaner 'n' bitin'
the postman every day—'spite him gettin' faster—
instead of every t'other day.
Like your pee gettin' stronger iffin you hold it awhile,
like when we go see Aunt Kate—
her outhouse bein' so fer away—and you hold it long and late.

Every time he crosses his legs, you see Daddy's legs
growin' knobbier and longer.
His hair's gettin' sparser and whiter.
Is he gettin' any stronger?

Mama's laugh got prettier, more sparklin'-like.
She said my freckles will go 'way an' my hair'll get curlier
and maybe even yellower, an' my boobs bigger, she say.
She taught me to bake biscuits flaky
and how to fry chicken tasty in hot lard.
Still, I'd believe her better if she was here in her sewing chair
an' not layin' up in the graveyard.

So if things get stronger as you get older,
will my tears keep stingin' more than my pee?
'Bout my freckles an' my hair an' my boobs? We'll see.

Stepping Stones

Pain and sorrow can age you fast,
But pain and sorrow don't have to last.

You square your shoulders, pray to the skies,
Goodness and beauty begin to arise.
Take in the colors of music and spheres,
Unstopped become your eyes and your ears.
Sway with the breeze, laugh with a friend.
Sorrow and pain are steps to an end.

Ephemera

Mayflies, poor things, live but a day,
mating having worn them out;
dragonflies last a bit longer—
perhaps their double wing construction prolongs their sojourn—
both, mayflies and dragonflies, go after having laid their eggs.
And centipedes, the dreaded thousand-leggers,
last even a shorter time, their eggs, that is,
if there's a spider nearby hungry.

Is there an Insect Heaven, for the so-called "lower life forms"?
Pastor Carl says dogs, especially the beloved ones,
no doubt go to heaven, where we can be re-united with them.

People—most of them—last a lot longer,
but they too go the way of the world.
They go to, some tell, out of this world,
and we wonder eternally: what's next?

I just hope, if there is an Insect Heaven,
I don't meet up with all the thousand-leggers I've stomped on.

After a Long Winter

Spring's coming. I know it!
My dog knows. He hops, skips,
chasing rabbit shadows dropped
on the brown grass.

Forsythia shoot fireworks into wintry skies,
birdsong melts icy winds, leaves uncoil,
stems swell, soon to birth
tulips, daffodils, insistent hyacinths.

Now **you** know! Love sweetens this mystery,
this work-in-progress, promising
this flower too will bloom.

April

Early in the month, early in the day, light green mists
drift and crown willow branches, fog erases treetops,
the pyrotechnics of forsythia remain,
spring flowers color hillsides,
points in a Seurat painting.

This afternoon, hyacinth bulbs—old-fashioned
colored Christmas tree lights—push through tired, thick,
multi-green crowns of leaves, breaking the soil.

I snip a few heavy stalks, diagonally,
as close to the leafcrowns as possible
so as not to injure them, then incise a few and put in a vase.

The scent of pink, lilac, white spears of tiny flowerets
leaves the living room palatial.

Next day, as I walk into the foyer, the scent overpowers.
Already the hyacinths are past their prime,
their waxy, fetid smell and faded blooms
overcome by soft, rotting leaves.

I move to toss them, debating whether I will cut more.
I clean the vase of its scum—no I won't,
yes I will, no—and put the vase into the dishwasher.

By evening when sundown has calmed scents down,
I turn the lamppost on and snip a few more, leaving
just a few to perfume the outside air.

s-t-r-e-t-c-h-i-n-g

first bend knees to chest,
then stretch out to the footboard,
bend ankles, wiggle toes
next reach arms for the headboard,
reach, reach and stretch, stretch
praying for hope, joy, expectancy
and all good things, including
safe driving and walking
and many holy encounters.

s-t-r-e-t-c-h b-o-d-y and S-o-u-l

Living Too Long

You've lived too long in the same development
when everyone knows you and beeps as they go by,
interrupting your steeping deep thoughts.
You wave pleasantly and smile,
then try to return to earlier reverie.
But they and the morning sun have intervened.
So you go home with just this poem to show for it.

Tai Chi

Eight years ago tai chi saved me from
a few nasty falls, after stumbling.
You learn to make your knees like jello
and the rest of your joints follow suit
so that if you trip, you maintain
balance even after ungraceful running
steps to save your face and slacks from
being torn by the sidewalk.

Two years later I repeated the course—
same instructor, same exercises.

Five years later I take it again, this time
developed by the Arthritis Association.
By now that disease and a very nasty fall
not caused by a sidewalk but a dishwasher door
have left me feeling a bit disabled yet,
bones having healed as much as they're going to.

The little old women and I (I'm still young)
wave our arms and hands in the air making clouds,
washing windows, and polishing tables.
We turn our ankles, hips, and knees into gelatin.
The teacher is excellent, not playing
Asian music but indoctrinating us
with Chris Botti's oldies melodies.

Today I almost fell as I almost did two
other times since Chris Botti.
As usual, it was an inch rise between cement blocks
while I was turning clouds to hippos and tortoises
and the skyline of New York City and wondering if
drainomaniphobia meant fear of turning
manicky over a clogged sink or disposal.

But my knees! my knees, turned into raspberry
jello, and I headed for home
perfectly relaxed about the whole situation.

New Things and Old Things

New things are beautiful:
    a gift-wrapped package with a surprise inside,
    an engine that purrs in a late-model car,
    the fresh smell of a just-sharpened pencil
    and first sight of a sparkling evening star.

Old things are beautiful:
    gnarled trees and shoes shaped to your feet,
    rough textue of an old barn's beams,
    grandmas with wrinkled skin and white hair,
    pebbles worn smooth by swift-moving streams.

Pianists

Rudolf Serkin playing glorious arpeggios
with the Philadelphia Orchestra at the Academy of Music,
Peter Nero at Wolftrap tickling the 88's,
Dave Brubeck pounding out syncopation.

From my friend Marjorie, a former classical pianist,
I've heard no glissandos.
The stroke has silenced her, for now.
Since she's not old in spirit, she may just tickle the ivories again.

Betty

Her grief was worse, having to make the hard,
hard decision, after murmurings didn't warn,
and collapse, shocking collapse, sent coma his way.

Brave, brave they were on the wings
of prayer, and all murmurings stopped.
Tears did not. Shared sorrow touched our telephone wires
and folding chairs in a church basement.

Many Cheez-Its and iced teas later we shared, too,
more tears, touch, time, and panic that takes your breath
that's taken by death.

Scaredy-Cats

No wonder we sturdy seniors fear more years,
what with golden turning into rusty,
hip, knee, shoulder replacement alloys now
infiltrating and making you more mobile.

Yet the presidents' promises
of at least eighty-percent Medicare boons fade
as our boom has faded.
Many of our secondaries are poor.
To get better pay-outs we have to sell off the arms and
legs we're trying to improve.

Our children may fare worse.
We worry about their future, too.
But with all the gym dates they keep,
they may keep the rust replacements at bay.
Hang in there, Kiddies. Medicare may not.

Faith

is doing the cross-word puzzle in ink,
the grocery list in ink and putting it in your purse
three days before going to Giant,
sure you needn't add anything,
and wondering why the pastor always
washes his hands after sharing the Peace.

Faith and Aging

When I get too old to pray, I'll die.

That's okay: who needs it then, when you're sitting in the Lap of Prayer.

Let the Good Times Roll

Walk twice a day in sunshine or rain.
Swim three-quarters of a mile
three or four times a week.
Eat broccoli and blueberries.
Breathe clean air.
Hire a housecleaner, but make your own bed.
Get seven to nine hours.
Wear bright lipstick
and put your hat on crooked sometimes.

And once in a while, roll out the barrel.

A Migraine's Prayer

Here I am in the recliner, Lord, the recliner and not the
bed,
here by the window beside the bed—
it's this darn pain in my head.
It started out as a tiny one, and then it escalated.
So tell me, Lord, tell me again why migraines were
created?

Tried aspirin, Lord, and Anacin—the caffeine seems to
help.
Excedrin's now the best, it seems, to stop this throbbing
hell.
Readin's out and typin' too,
so what's a gal to do?

It's only two a.m., I see, so it will last till seven.
Usually five hours is all it takes.
Lord, please take me to heaven!

(Do You mind a little assistance from Excedrin?)

Mammogram

This day the garment, the one that opens down the front,
is not blue but salmon, a good sign.
I look down at my "girls" and say,
"This won't take long or hurt much."

The technologist has thoughtfully warmed with a heating pad
the plates (see, girls, I told you this wouldn't be so bad—
though it does hurt like heck, my pain memory being keen),
and tells me, with a smile, to wait while she makes sure
the films came out okay.

Soon, the smile not so bright, she enters the room:
"The doctor would like me to take some more.
There's just a shadow . . ."

"You know I had a cyst removed from the one twenty years
ago . . . ?"

"Yes, it's not likely that. Here, maybe it won't hurt this time."

"Ouch! Sorry, I'll try to be brave . . ."

"Ouch!" "Sorry."

"The radiologist would like you to come back
for an ultra-sound in three to four days . . ."

(Don't you notify my family doctor first with the report?

Why such a hurry?

Oh, God, there's not been any cancer in my family!

Three to four days of hell, pure hell.)

"Could I see what he's concerned about?"

She puts the film on the lighted screen
and points out the pea-sized dark spot.

"Couldn't it be a cyst, too?"

"Probably is, darling. Don't worry,
just make your appointment on your way out."

So, it is pure hell, during which I frantically call my beloved Dr. B.
whose nurse says to make the appointment after the ultra-sound, and
talk to numerous girlfriends—"Did you ever have this happen? Did
you ever *hear* of this happening?"

No one had.

The ultra-sound is interesting (I always learn something
from such things), as the technician explains every step.
He moves the screen so I can watch
as the wand moves 'round and' round.

"I don't see anything. What should I look for?"
"Whatever's there," he answers,
meaning whatever unusual is there.
However, "There is nothing unusual," the tech says.
"The radiologist will read it, but I can tell you, it's okay.
You still need to have the exam from Dr. B.
We'll fax the report to him today."
"Sometimes I feel it and sometimes I can't," I tell Dr. B.
He says, "I don't feel it—ah, yes, it's there, but—."
He palpates gently a bit more. "It's nothing, I'm sure.
Probably a small cyst."
"So what do we do? I've been told by an MRI tech
I should get a needle biopsy regardless of results."
"You could," he says. "But I'd advise waiting
till your next mammogram.
Schedule one for three months—if you can live with that.
See me in a month."
I pray and decide I can live with that.
Three months is not as long as three minutes when you're sure
the jaws of hell are waiting to swallow you.

Chemotherapy

It's a lot like riding a roller coaster: your stomach drops,
your hair blows in the wind—your hair, soon to disappear?—
who knows.
Who knows what it's like to feel trapped and so scared,
except other cancer SURVIVORS.

Patience

We think of the photographer with his multiple telephoto lenses
and many filters waiting for the blue heron to step
one-half inch into the sunlight where his velvet plume
would turn to satin . . .

We snapped our memories and left before it turned,
being satisfied with velvet.

Phases

First a few gray hairs you pluck, wrinkles you smooth with cream.
Then a creaky knee on a rainy day, a name or word that escapes.
Character lines begin to look like a road map
and you stop plucking, else you'll go bald.
"I'm getting older," you think, and summon determination
and a plan: more fruits and veggies and fish, One-a-Day vitamins,
bike or walk a mile every day.

Eyes and ears fail, and doctor appointments outnumber
your grandkids' pictures on the refrigerator door.
You think, "Old age is no fun," and commiserate with peers.
Then come A-fibs or V-fibs and angina
and short term memory shot to heck.
Rust in all your joints: Ben-Gay overwhelms Arpege or Old Spice,
depending on how many joints you slather it on.
You lose some weight, exercise when it's sunny,
and complete the daily crossword puzzle.
"I feel old," you say to yourself on bad days.
"I *am* old," you say out loud as you move from cane to walker—
praying the wheelchair's only temporary—
while the kitchen table overflows with medications
and more supplements.

Calendar pages flip faster and faster, and you barely recognize
your graduation photo. These days more people in obituaries
are younger than you.
You shout to the world loudly and a bit proudly,
"I am an *old* old person."

You avoid the alphabet soup of MS, ALS, RA, CA, CAD,

unless you're under the hill before you go over it.

Suffering is inevitable, some say, but *misery is optional*.
   Summon faith and hope,
      courage, resilience, patience,
         perhaps even some elegance.
Go boldly. Exit smiling.

The New Olympics

I heard the Olympics Committee is considering a category
for video gaming. I think they should create a category
for old people called Knitting if they really want to see fingers fly!

No Dieting

I'm putting on a little more weight than usual,
reserve in case something comes up and hits me in the face again—
like usual.

Lifeblood

There are some poems I don't have to write.
Someone has already written them:
Shakespeare, cummings, D. Thomas, Angelou, Mary Oliver,
Billy Collins, and other Poet Laureates already did the job.
It's heavy lifting sometimes—like preaching or gardening—
hard on the head, the heart, the hand.

But as long as I hear music, I guess I'll have to warble
like the cardinal outside my window.
As long as my cardiac system works, my eyes see the light,
my hand holds a pencil—
the earth keeps on beating—
the words keep on coming.

50-100-1000

Everyone has 50-100-1000 sense songs buried,
waiting to bubble to the surface.
Can we—can you?—stand the red hot pokers
stabbing in the dark, and bring them to light?

On Writing

Feel the leather, turn on lights. try words, hear sounds.
Chisel an idea, dive to the bottom of the well, harvest sense-seeds
from growth and death, return the incarnate to spirit,
give back the gifts, shape, make music, order with feeling.

A Place to Live

Abraham's folks had it, the land of milk and honey.
    They lost that land but gained another when Jeremiah
    said it was hearts, not tablets of stone that were important.
    The carpenter—he hung from a wooden tree—
    promised a mansion.
We work for dream houses (with mortgage
    and insurance payments, fuel bills, repairs)
    or a piece of land out in the country, or we,
    the mobile generation of the New (Promised Land) World,
    yearn to go home again, to our birthplace.
Meanwhile beams hewn by the lathe of love
    and chisel of truth build a shelter of faith, firm, unyielding,
    yet yielding much in promises.
    We push against those beams and they never go away—
    unless *we* leave them.
    Above, around, beyond, within, we find that empty tomb:
we—and not so darkly—see the Promised Land.

Peaceable Kingdom: Insects, Arachnids and Annelids

I like spiders because they eat thousand-legger eggs.
I hate thousand-leggers: stepped on one once in my bare feet!
It troubles me that cockroaches will inherit the earth.
Are they that meek?

Sometimes I hesitated to garden when my trowel
kept cutting earthworms in half.
But I did it anyway, the trowel my plowshare-into-sword
when I was angry.
Then one day I heard that a half-earthworm grows into a whole,
a new head or tail, whatever is required.
This was good news, as earthworms till the soil, keep it friable,
loose and free, so roots can drink water and nitrogen,
thus perpetuating life.
I was freed from guilt by knowledge of this miracle.

Why was it sinful to eat of the Tree of Knowledge?
While knowledge can mean good or evil, if *we're* to regenerate,
we choose Good.

Heaven, if there is one, is not pearly gates and golden streets,
I hope. I hope we're let back into that profusion of maples and
pomegranates
and seedless grapes and butter-and-cream corn,
dahlias and daffodils, lilacs, azaleas and mock orange.
Bats and cows and beetles and bees and Golden Retrievers,
congregations of snow geese, alley cats and strays and runaways.
Plantains and coolies and all my loves and visiting angels—
we race to them all with joy,
each with open arms for that heavenly embrace.

Oh, and of course earthworms.
Please, God, no cockroaches. Just spiders and thousand-leggers
lying down together.

Too Soon

Already we're feeling refreshing September
in the middle of August, the trees full of buzzing locusts,
the mums blooming now, next to the zinnias.
I wonder if I'll have them for the Thanksgiving table.

Walking, I imagine snow already crunching on the concrete.
I hope my neighbor's pink roses spill sugar into the air
in the middle of December as they did last year.
I wonder, were they too soon or too late?

What Did You Do Today?

Haydn wrote over a hundred symphonies.
Mozart wrote five hundred beauties before thirty-three,
and Keats "The Eve of St. Agnes," "Endymion,"
"Ode to a Grecian Urn," and other lovely odes
before his death at twenty-six.

Did you put some rivets in a skyscraper?
write "Well done" on a term paper?
rock a baby to sleep?
draw a picture-map for someone lost?
teach a first-grader how to spell "cat"? take a teacher to lunch?
find a rabbit in the clouds?

Life

Considering it a race to be won
battle to be fought
or gift to be shared
makes all the difference.

CPSIA information can be obtained at www.ICGtesting.com
Printed in the USA
BVOW08s1347311213

340596BV00001BA/16/P

9 781491 841617